MW00387722

The
Gutenberg
Bible

THE EARLIEST
PORTRAIT OF JOHANN GUTENBERG
This engraving,
presumably an imaginary likeness,
shows a man with a forked beard and
a furred cap, with a die of twelve letters
of the alphabet in his left hand. It first
appeared in a book by André Thevet,
Paris, 1584.

The
Gutenberg
Bible

Landmark in Learning

James Thorpe

❖ Huntington Library ❖

San Marino, California

LIBRARY OF CONGRESS CATALOGING
IN PUBLICATION DATA
Thorpe, James Ernest, 1915–The Gutenberg Bible:
Landmark in Learning / by James Thorpe.
p. cm.   ISBN: 0-87328-169-1
1. Gutenberg Bible.
2. Incunabula—Germany—Mainz (Rhineland-Palatinate)
3. Printing—Germany—Mainz (Rhineland-Palatinate)-
History—Origin and antecedents.   I. Title.
z241.B58T47   1998   093—dc21   97-38318
CIP

Back Cover Detail:
ILLUMINATED INITIAL "P" AND MARGINAL DECORATIONS
BEGINNING OF THE BOOK OF PROVERBS, OLD TESTAMENT

Above:
ILLUMINATED INITIAL "E",
BEGINNING OF THE BOOK OF LAMENTATIONS, OLD TESTAMENT

Front Cover and Contents page:
ILLUMINATED INITIAL "M",
ILLUSTRATING AN ANGEL, THE SYMBOL OF MATTHEW
NEW TESTAMENT • PROLOGUE TO THE BOOK OF MATTHEW

Pages 7-8
ILLUMINATED INITIAL "F" AND MARGINAL DECORATIONS
BEGINNING OF THE BOOK OF I KINGS, OLD TESTAMENT

The body text is Adobe Minion,
a typeface designed by Robert Slimbach.
Minion is inspired by classical, oldstyle typefaces of the
late Renaissance, a period of highly readable type designs.

The display type on the cover and title pages
is Monotype Truesdell, the 47th typeface of F.W. Goudy.
The original font was destroyed in a fire but this
digitized version was created by Steve Matteson in 1993
using Goudy's original letterpress proofs.

Printed in Singapore by C.S. Graphics on 170 gsm Multi-art silk.

Contents

libros diuisus ē. ſtōnus teſter. Atꝗ
ita ſūt pīter veteris legis libri viginti
duo: id ē moyſi quiꝗ: et ꝑphaꝝ octo:
agiog̃ĵphoꝝ noue̅. Quāuis̃ nōnulli
ruth: ꝉ einoch inter agiographa ſcrip
titent: ꝉ ipſ libros ī ſuo putet numeo
ſupputādos: ac ꝑ hoc eſſe priſce legis
libros viginti̅ꝗtuor quos ſub nume
ro vigīti̅quatuor ſenioꝝ apocalipſis
iohis inducit· adorantes agnu̅· et co
ronas ſuas ꝓſtratis vultib3 offere̅tes
ſta̅tib3 cora̅ ꝗtuor aīalib3 oculatis
ante et retro id eſt in ꝑteritu̅ ꝉ in futuꝝ
reſpicietib3· et indefeſſa voce clama̅
bus·ſanctus·ſc̅s·ſc̅s·dn̅s deus omni
potens· qui erat· ꝉ qui eſt· ꝉ qui ve̅tur9
eſt. hic ꝓlogus ſcripturaꝝ quaſi ga
leatū principiū· ōnib3 libris quos de
hebreo ve̅timus9 ī latinu̅ cōuenire poteſt:
ut ſcire valeamus9 quitqd extra hos eſt·
inter apocrapha ē̅ ponendū. Igitur
ſapia ꝗ vulgo ſalomois̃ inſcribit· et
ihu ſilij ſirach lib3 ꝉ iudich· ꝉ thobias·
ꝉ paſtor nō ſūt ī canone. Machabeoꝝ
ꝑmū libru̅· hebraicū repꝑi. Sed3 ſecūs gree9
ē̅: qd ex ipſa phraſy ꝓbari poteſt. Que
cū ita ſe habeā: obſecro te lector· ne la
borem meu̅ repheſione̅ eſtimes anti
quoꝝ. Ju tēplo dei· offert unuſquiſꝗ
qd poteſt. Alij aurū ꝉ argentu̅ ꝉ lapi
des ꝑcioſos· alij biſſū ꝉ purpuram ꝉ
coccū offerūt ꝉ iacintū. ſtobiſcū bene
agitur· ſi obtulerimus9 pelles ꝉ capraꝝ
pilos. Et tame̅ apls̃ ꝯtemptibiliora
nr̅a magis neceſſaria iudicat. Unde
et tota illa tabernacli pulchritudo· et
ꝑ ſingulas ſpecies eccl̅e ꝓntis· futureꝗ3
diſtincɔ pallib3 regit ꝉ cilicijs: ardore
ꝗ ſolis· ꝉ iniuriā vmbriū· ea ꝗ viſio
ra ſūt ꝓhibet. Lege ergo ꝑmū ſamuel.

et malachim meū. Meū inꝗ
Quitꝗd enī crebrius vertendo
dando ſollicicius· ꝉ didicimus9
nr̅m ē. Et cū intellexis qd au
bas· ut interꝑtem me eſtimas
es· ut paraſraſten ſi ingratu̅
michi omino ꝯſcius nō ſum
me quippiā de hebraica veꝛit̅a
ſi incredulus es· lege grecos ꝉ
latios· ꝉ ꝯfer cū hijs opuſcul
emendauimus9· ꝉ vbicūꝗ3 diſcre
ſe videris· interroga quelibet
cui magis accomodare debe
et ſi noſtra firmauerit· puto
eſtimes ꝛetortorem· ut ī eode̅ l
ſiliter diuinarit. Sed ꝉ vos ꝝ
xp̅i rogo ꝗ dn̅i diſcubitis pec
fideū mirra vngitis caput· ꝗ
ſaluatore queritis ī ſepulchꝛ
iā ad preiu̅ xp̅e aſcedit· ut ꝯt
res canes· qui aduerſū me re
deſeuiūt· et circueūt ciuitate̅
ſe doctos arbitrant ſi alijs d
oracionum vr̅aꝝ clippeos oꝑ
Ego ſciens humilitate̅ mea̅
ſeuterie recordabor. Dixi ī
vias meas· ut nō delinqua̅
mea. Poſui ori meo custod
ſiſteret peccator aduiſū me. L
et humiliat9 ſū: ꝉ ſilui de bon

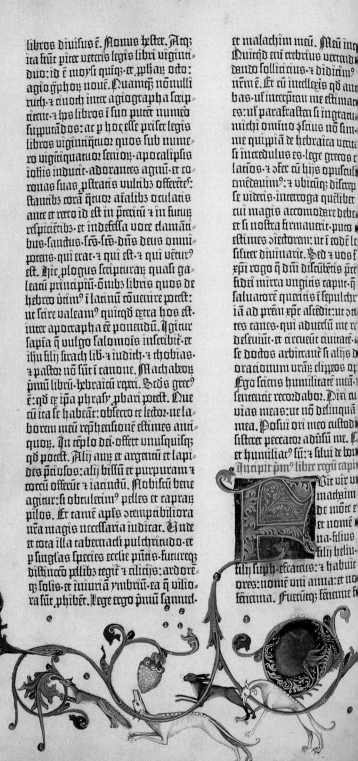

Jncipit ꝑm9 liber regū rapi

Vit vir i
machaim
de mōte e
et nome
na·filius
ſilij heliu̅
ſilij ſuph· efrateus· ꝉ habuit
ores· nomē vni anna· et no
fēcenna. Fueruntꝗ3 ſēcenne ſi

[col. 1]

...rãt liberi. Et ascendebat vir
...itate sua statutis diebus: ut a...
...sacrificaret dño exercituũ in...
...at aũt ibi duo filij heli. oftni...
...acerdotes dñi. Venit ergo dies...
...it helchana. deditque senienne...
...et cũctis filijs eius et filiabus...
...Anne autem dedit partem vnã...
...nia annam diligebat. Dñs...
...iserat vuluã ei?. Affligebat...
...emula eius. et vehementer an...
...tanũ ut exprobraret cp dñs...
...e vuluã eius. Sicque faciebat...
...s ãnos. cũque redeunte tpe ascede...
...plũ dñi: et sic puocabat eã...
...la flebat: et nõ capiebat cibũ...
...et helchana vir suus. Anna...
...ere nõ comedis: et quãobre...
...or tuis? Nũqd nõ ego melior...
...iã dece filijs? Surrexit auteñ...
...ostqp comederat et biberat in...
...ich sacerdote sedere sup sellã...
...res domꝰ dñi: cũ esset anna...
...animo: orauit ad dñm flẽs...
...et votũ vouit dicens. Dñe ex...
...respiciẽs videas afflicconem...
...ue: et recordat? mei fueris nec...
...ancille tue. Dederisque serue tue...
...e dabo eũ dño omnibus diebus...
...et nouacula nõ ascendet sup...
...8. factũ est aũt cũ illa mltĩ...
...ces corã dño: ut hely obser...
...eius. Porro anna loquebat...
...quo: tantũque labia eius moue...
...vox penitus nõ audiebatur...
...sit ergo eam hely temulentã...
...d. Vsquequo ebria eris? Dige...
...inũ quo mades. Respondes...
...equasi inqt dñe mi. Nã nn...
...e nimis ego sum: vinũque et...

[col. 2]

...que quod inebriare potest non bibi. sed
effudi animã meã in cõspectu dñi. Ne
reputes ancillã tuã quasi vnã de filiabus
belial. quia ex multitudine doloris et
meroris mei locuta sũ usque in presens.
Tunc hely ait ei. Vade in pace. et deus
isrl det tibi peticonem tuã quã rogasti
eũ. Et illa dixit. Vtinã inueniat an-
cilla tua gratiã in oculis tuis. Et abijt
mulier in viã suã et comedit: vultusque
illiꝰ nõ sut ãplius in diuersa mutari.
Et surrexerunt mane. et adorauerunt
corã dño: reuersique sũt et venerũt in
domũ suã ramatha. Cognouit aũt
helchana annã vxorem suã: et recordat?
est eiꝰ dñs. Et factũ est post circulũ dierũ
cõcepit anna et peperit filiũ: vocauitque
nomẽ eius samuel: eo cp a dño postu-
lasset eũ. Ascẽdit aũt vir eiꝰ helchana
et oĩs domꝰ eiꝰ: ut immolaret dño hostiã
solennẽ: et votũ suũ: et anna nõ ascen-
dit. Dixit enim viro suo. Non vadam
donec ablactetur infans: et ducã eũ ut
appareat ante cõspectũ dñi: et maneat
ibi iugiter. Et ait ei helchana vir suus.
Fac quod bonũ tibi videtur: et mane
donec ablactes eũ: precorque ut impleat
dñs verbũ tuũ. Mansit ergo mulier
et lactauit filiũ suũ: donec amoueret
eũ a lacte. Et adduxit eũ secũ postqp ab-
lactauerat in vitulis tribus et tribus mo-
dijs farine et ãphora vini: et adduxit
eũ ad domũ dñi in silo. Puer autem
erat adhuc infantulus. Et immolaue-
runt vitulũ: et obtulerũt puerũ hely. Et
ait anna. Obsecro mi dñe: viuit aĩa
tua dñe. Ego sum illa mulier que steti
corã te hic: orãs dñm pro puero isto.
Orationem dedit michi dñs peticonem
meã quã postulaui eũ. Idcirco et ego

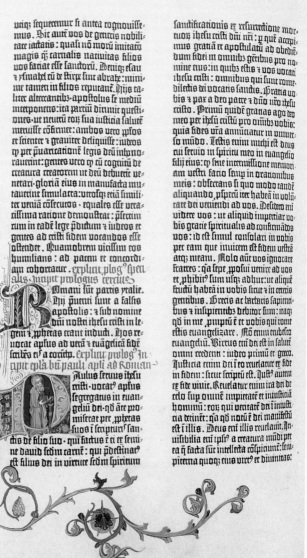

ILLUMINATED INITIAL "P"
AND MARGINAL DECORATIONS
BEGINNING OF THE BOOK OF ROMANS
NEW TESTAMENT

❖ I ❖

Introduction

RARELY HAS fame ever been so well placed as that which surrounds the Gutenberg Bible. This noble book, which appeared about 1455, has long been taken to represent the invention of printing in the western world. In that role, it symbolizes one of the small handful of the greatest human accomplishments of all time. It can be considered along with such great ancient achievements as writing and numeration, along with such great modern achievements as the steam engine and the use of electricity. Sometimes the importance of an invention—or of any human act—lies in what it leads to. It can truly be said that the invention of printing from movable metal type, in Germany in the middle of the fifteenth century, led to a radical change in the whole world of the intellect. It is this great invention that we are considering through the symbol of a single book, the Gutenberg Bible. Let us first take a look at the consequences of this invention from the perspectives of people living in Europe in the middle of the fifteenth century.

Books were available, but their text was of course written by hand. Today we sometimes think that all books are printed, and that texts written by hand should be called manuscripts. So they may, but the term "book" existed long before printing, and its meanings include any set of leaves, whether written or printed, that are bound together. Before printing, the making of a book was a laborious process, full of chances for error. It might take one scribe a full year to copy a single long book. Consequently books were very scarce and very expensive, and they were full of mistakes that the copyist had inevitably made in the course of his work.

Libraries existed in only a few centers of learning. In England at that time the abbey libraries at Canterbury and Bury were among the largest, with some 2,000 books each, but the Cambridge University Library had only 300, and very few learned men had any books at all. The most common books were Bibles, collections of psalms, and other books for religious services, almost entirely in Latin; after these, the most numerous books were writings from classical antiquity.

Although books were scarce, education was much more widespread in the later Middle Ages than is sometimes supposed. By 1450, in some areas of England for which there is evidence, up to thirty or forty percent of the adults were literate—that is, they could read. Writing was something separate, taught as an artisan skill, like shoemaking, with the rest of the literate world left to scribble as best it could. Hence our feeling, from looking at their handwriting, that great writers and notable personages of those times must have been partially illiterate and therefore probably stupid—such is our vanity that we can always turn to our own advantage a comparison between ourselves and talented people of the distant past.

There were many kinds of schooling available in England in the middle of the fifteenth century, and most children could get at least a rudimentary education, whatever their social or financial condition. Grammar schools (for the fortunate few) offered the best education, and the rich had tutors for their children. But there was also a multitude of small and often informal parish schools taught by the clergy: the lesser clergy operated what were called chantry schools (associated with chapels for chanting masses), and even in tiny villages the priests or clerks taught the children of the parish. Learning was increasingly valued, and about this time the guilds of skilled artisans began to introduce minimum standards of education for membership. The Goldsmiths' Company, for example, passed a rule that no apprentice could be taken "without he can write and read."

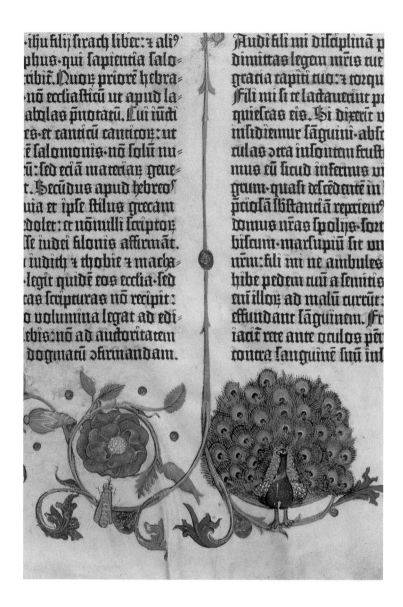

MARGINAL DECORATIONS

BEGINNING OF THE BOOK OF PROVERBS

OLD TESTAMENT

The invention of printing provided books in abundance to serve the varieties of established schooling and to satisfy the hunger for learning. There was, in fact, a veritable explosion of books, an explosion heard around the western world. In the forty-five years after the Gutenberg Bible—through 1501, that is—more than ten million books had been printed, being copies of forty thousand different works. It would have taken all the copyists in Europe at least a thousand years to have turned out the books printed in those forty-five years. And that was only the merest beginning, the production of the years now called the incunable period, or the cradle of printing. When the invention outgrew its swaddling clothes, its effects really began to be felt. By 1501 there were 1,120 printing offices in 260 different towns in 17 European countries, and their output of printed books outran belief.

The result was a series of revolutions in learning, first, in the dissemination and increase of knowledge. Vastly more material became available for education in schools and for self-education. Earlier, teaching had been mainly oral; afterward, learning came mainly from reading. Those who were literate became very much more learned, and many achieved a depth of learning which only a few had ever before possessed. From this came an explosion of knowledge, the creation of new knowledge on a scale that had never before been imagined. Before then, the principal way of creating new knowledge had been through analysis of a limited number of authorities, primarily scripture and writings of classical antiquity. Free access to a greater body of knowledge was an important stimulant to creativity of other kinds, including experimental work. At the same time, the human intellect itself underwent a radical change in its adaptation to the demands of a very much greater body of knowledge and of new ways to deal with it, to use it, and to increase it.

The other revolution was a radical change in our social and political order as a result of a great increase in literacy. For a time, the literacy rate changed only rather slowly after the invention of printing. Education (of which literacy is a simple symptom) has generally had, at least from a large body of English-speaking peoples, a mixed reaction of awe and suspicion, as a state to be admired from a safe distance. Literacy gradually increased, however, because of the availability of the printed book and thanks to some legal nudges. Probably about thirty or forty percent of the adults in England were literate in the sixteenth and seventeenth centuries, approximately sixty percent in the eighteenth century, and perhaps ninety percent in our own time. The tremendous consequences of the increase in literacy were that it made democracy possible on more than a local level, and that it led to a social ordering on the bases of education and intellectual achievement, in addition to the earlier bases of wealth and family position. Thus it was that the invention of printing had a mighty influence, in crucial ways, on the development of the world as we know it today.

ILLUMINATED INITIAL "P"

ILLUSTRATING ST. PAUL

NEW TESTAMENT · BOOK OF ROMANS

ILLUMINATED INITIAL "I"
AND MARGINAL DECORATIONS ILLUSTRATING CREATION
OLD TESTAMENT · BOOK OF GENESIS

⁘ II ⁘

The Emergence of Printing
and the Gutenberg Bible

H ow did the invention of printing come to pass and how was the Gutenberg Bible produced? Most statements about the invention of printing are carefully limited to Europe and to movable type; these statements leave a considerable part of the globe unaccounted for and an indefinite number of other methods of printing unbespoken. Let me first indicate the reasons for these reservations.

The two historical methods of printing are block printing, and printing from movable type. In block printing, the outlines of words or pictures are carved on a block of wood, and an impression is made by inking the block and pressing a piece of paper (or vellum) on it. The disadvantages of block printing are numerous: the carving is very slow handwork, the outlines are relatively crude, the blocks wear out, and it is difficult to print from large blocks or from combinations of blocks. Printing from movable type involves placing individual letters or characters into lines (composing), adding lines until the desired page is full, and using a press to transfer ink to paper from a number of these pages at the same time. The advantages of printing from movable metal type were, at the outset, that it was fast, cheap, and clear; the type could be uniform, of any size desired, reusable, and capable of producing a relatively large number of impressions without wearing out.

Block printing existed before printing from movable type. The earliest dated European woodblock print is dated 1423; it is a picture, without words, of St. Christopher bearing the infant Christ. It is only a guess that wood-block printing was common in early times; all the extant European block books—blocks with

17

text, that is—seem to be slightly later than the Gutenberg Bible, and the method died in the sixteenth century.

The earliest printed book known is a ninth-century Chinese wood-block printing of the Diamond Sutra in the form of a roll sixteen feet long and one foot wide, made by pasting together the impressions from a series of wood blocks. There was considerable block printing in China. Marco Polo the wide-eyed traveler from Venice who visited China in the thirteenth century, tells of the marvelous Chinese printed money—black money on paper made from the bark of the mulberry tree, with the official seal on it in red ink. It was made by block printing. Probably Marco Polo's wonder lay mostly in the opportunity that the ruler thus had to produce unlimited wealth for himself, a possibility we still have with us, still called "printing press money."

It was in China also that we first hear of printing from movable type, in the eleventh century. The type was made of pieces of clay baked until hard, and the impression was taken by placing the paper on the type, apparently without the use of a press. (In Korea in the fifteenth century some type was made from copper and books were printed from it for a time.) The nature of the Chinese language inhibited the development of printing from movable type, however. Our basic alphabet has twenty-six characters, with constant repetition and hence both economy and manageability in reusing type. The Chinese language, with some forty thousand ideographs, was so ill-adapted to take advantage of movable type that printing never really developed in China in the early period. The Chinese experience had, in fact, no apparent influence on the invention of printing in Europe.

The Chinese invention that was influential, however, was paper making. By the end of the first century of the Christian era, the Chinese had developed the making of paper, using treebark, hemp, rags, even old fish nets. The alleged inventor was Ts'ai Lun, a eunuch at the court of the emperor. Ts'ai Lun met his end in a striking manner: when he could not find his way out of a squab-

ILLUMINATED INITIAL "O"
BEGINNING OF THE BOOK OF MALACHI
OLD TESTAMENT

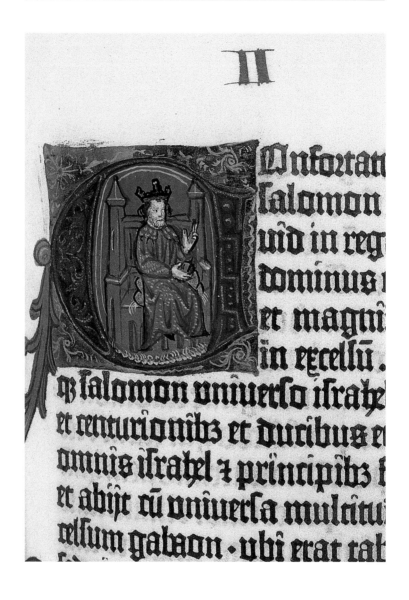

ILLUMINATED INITIAL "C"
BEGINNING OF THE BOOK OF II CHRONICLES
OLD TESTAMENT

ble between himself, the empress, and the emperor's grand-mother, he went home, took a bath, combed his hair, put on his best clothes, and drank poison! His invention reached the Near East in the eighth century and came to Europe, through Spain, in the twelfth and thirteenth centuries.

The availability of inexpensive paper was crucial to the development of printing. The other requirements were a suitable metal alloy that could be used for type, and a machine that would cast uniform metal type speedily. With this preamble, the stage is set for the introduction of Johann Gutenberg, the invention of printing, and the Gutenberg Bible.

Our main sources of information on these subjects are twenty-eight legal documents which have been discovered in the course of the last five centuries. Several of them are lawsuits—unfortunately for Gutenberg, but fortunately for us, as even then lawsuits involved the recitation of background facts and the testimony of witnesses. Still, many matters about his life, about the invention of printing, and about the production of the book we call the Gutenberg Bible are far from clear, and there is room for dispute on large as well as small points. I will not explore those disputes but give a general account based on the primary documents and provide, for doubtful issues, the best scholarly consensus, so far as there is one. Learned men are no less contentious than the rest of the world, and small matters tend to rouse large passions.

Johann Gutenberg was born in the prosperous German city of Mainz, on the Rhine River, about the year 1399, or within the preceding five years. His family was formally classed, according to the ordering of the day, as "patrician," and they were prosperous, owning property and having income from annuities. Gutenberg was not content to live the usual life of a patrician, however. He seems to have been a restless man who probed into various new possibilities. He was something of a projector, bold and venturesome. He also had a strong will and a strong temper.

He early learned the craft of the goldsmith—though it was unusual for one in his social class to do so. When he was about twenty-nine, in 1428, Mainz was divided by a conflict between the artisans and the patricians. The artisans won, and Gutenberg had to go into exile; he went to Strasbourg, about a hundred and fifty miles up the Rhine.

There he moved in aristocratic circles and came to know a patrician woman named Ennelin zur Isernen Türe, and they planned to be married. Gutenberg apparently decided to back out, however, and the lady promptly brought suit against him for breach of promise. In the ecclesiastical court, a citizen named Claus Schott gave testimony against Gutenberg, which testimony (as the report went) "Gutenberg contradicted and rejected, declaring deponent to be a miserable wretch who lived by cheating and lying." For these utterances, Schott brought another suit against Gutenberg for the use of defamatory language, and he received provisional damages. How the breach of promise suit came out, we do not know; but eight years later the lady was still unmarried, and Gutenberg appears to have remained a bachelor for the rest of his life.

It was in Strasbourg that Gutenberg's restless mind started him on a career as an inventor and manufacturer. He developed a method for polishing precious stones. He worked out a way to manufacture mirrors, at a time when mirrors were uncommon and expensive. His experiments were doubtless costly, both in materials and in establishing a shop with skilled workmen. So he went into partnership with two other people, who contributed large sums of money in return for being taught what Gutenberg called his "secret arts." Their first plan was to make some special hand mirrors to sell to pilgrims going to Aachen (Aix-la-Chapelle) in 1439. When the pilgrimage was postponed for a year, the partners urged Gutenberg to teach them his other "secret art," which may have been printing. But it may just as well have been related to his work with pilgrim's mirrors.

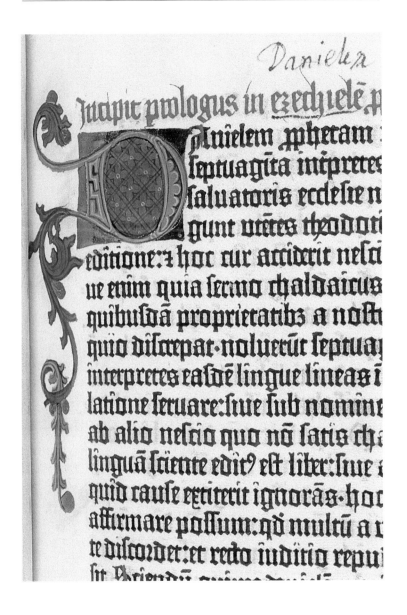

ILLUMINATED INITIAL "D" AND MARGINAL DECORATIONS
BEGINNING OF THE PROLOGUE TO THE BOOK OF DANIEL
OLD TESTAMENT

ILLUMINATED INITIAL "P"
ILLUSTRATING ST. PETER
NEW TESTAMENT · BOOK OF I PETER

When one of the partners died, Gutenberg entered into lit-igation rather than let someone else learn his "secret arts." Harsh words were passed between the partners. Gutenberg's servant complained that a partner accused him of lying and that the partner also (in the words of the suit) "shouted to me publicly: 'Listen, soothsayer, you must tell the truth for me, even if I should get upon the gallows with you'; and thus he maliciously accused and charged me with being a perjured villain, whereby he did me injustice before the grace of God, which surely are very evil things."

Such partnerships do not seem destined to last forever, and this one expired legally in 1443. In the next year, Gutenberg was able to return to Mainz after an absence of some fifteen years. I do not know whether he was able to take the contents of his wine cel-lar with him or not; if so, it was quite a move, as, according to the tax record, it contained some 420 gallons. He continued his work on printing in Mainz for the next dozen years, until 1455, when the printing of the Gutenberg Bible was completed.

Being an inventor can be impoverishing, and being an entrepreneur may be bankrupting, particularly when almost all the financial entries are on the outgo pages and virtually none on the income ones. Gutenberg had very ambitious plans, and he exhausted his own funds in the first few years of his enterpris-ing; thereafter he had to embark on the risky course of borrowing money which he hoped to repay from the uncertain returns of an indefinite future. He was carrying the interest (at 5%) on a loan that he had made in 1442 from the Parish of St. Thomas in Stras-bourg; in 1448 he borrowed 150 guilders in Mainz, using a rela-tive as security; in 1450 he had to borrow the very large sum of 800 guilders (at 6% interest) from a lawyer-capitalist-goldsmith named Johann Fust in order "to finish the work." But in two years, that money was gone, too, and he went back to Fust for an-other 800 guilders; this time the prudent Fust insisted on becom-ing a partner in the enterprise in order to protect his investment.

In the meantime, the experiments with printing were going forward. Several fonts of type were designed, a metal alloy was developed, a machine to cast type was invented, ink was worked out from the formula for oil paint introduced for painting some twenty years before by Jan van Eyck, and the press was perfected. About a dozen different works from this experimental period have been identified—often in fragmentary form as waste paper found in the binding of other books—and it is assumed that they were done by Gutenberg or his associates. Perhaps the earliest one, printed between 1442 and 1454, is a tiny fragment of one leaf of a poem, in German, on the "World Judgment"; it is calculated, from this fragment, that the whole poem would have run to about seventy-four pages. There are fragments of various editions of a Latin grammar by Donatus. The earliest dated work (1454) is a Papal Indulgence, in several different issues; and there is a twelve-page leaflet, "A Warning to Christendom against the Turks"—timely in view of the fact that Constantinople had fallen the year before—concluding with the earliest printed New Year's greeting, for the year 1455: "Eyn gut selig nuwe Jar."

1455 proved to be a good but not a happy New Year for Gutenberg. It was a good year in that the printing of the Bible was finished. The text of the Bible is in Latin, in the version called the Vulgate, prepared by St. Jerome in the fourth century and in common use in the Roman Catholic Church. The version printed by Gutenberg was from a very accurate copy of the Paris revision, prepared by biblical scholars in the thirteenth century. (The Vulgate is still sometimes thought of as the "Roman Catholic Bible"; when Harry S. Truman took the oath of office as President of the United States in 1949, a peaceful balance was maintained by using two Bibles: a small English one for a Protestant Bible, and a facsimile of the Gutenberg Bible for a Catholic Bible.)

The printing of the Gutenberg Bible was indeed a mon-

Illuminated Initial "V"
Beginning of the Book of Zephaniah
Old Testament

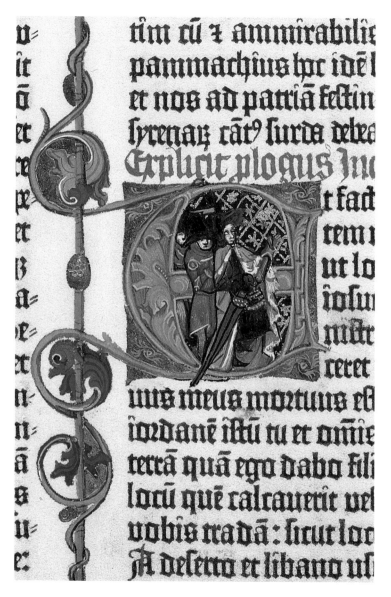

ILLUMINATED INITIAL "E"
BEGINNING OF THE BOOK OF JOSHUA
OLD TESTAMENT

28

umental task. It was set in type which had been designed to imitate handwriting. There were several different forms of handwriting in use by copyists. The specific form of handwriting which was the model for the type of this book was, naturally enough, the one in common use in Western Germany in the middle of the fifteenth century, called gothic. The type based on it is called gothic, or black letter.

The type of the Gutenberg Bible was designed and cast for this job, and the text was composed in two columns to the page and forty-two lines to the column; hence it is sometimes called "the forty-two line Bible," though a few of the earlier pages set were in forty or forty-one lines. The complete Bible totals some 1,282 folio pages. At first, four compositors worked on it, then six; it is estimated that six compositors devoted two full years to typesetting alone. The printing began with one press, but soon six presses were in use; even so, it must have taken about two full years to see the sheets through the press. It is thought that something like one hundred and thirty-five copies were printed on paper, and forty copies on vellum. It must have been a good year for Gutenberg.

The reason that 1455 was not a happy year for Gutenberg was that his financial house of cards fell down. The amount of capital needed to produce the Bible was enormous. There was the large cost of tools, equipment, wages, and of the experimental work during the preceding decade or more. Moreover, the paper and vellum for the Bible alone would have been a big investment; it is estimated that more than 5,000 calfskins were required for the forty copies on vellum, and the equivalent of more than 50,000 sheets of paper 16½ × 12 inches for the one hundred and thirty-five copies on paper. (The paper would, in practice, have presumably been in the form of some 25,000 sheets twice the size of the leaves of the book, with two pages being printed on each side and the sheet folded once before binding; thus were two leaves, or a total of four printed pages, created in folio from each sheet of paper.) Of course all this material had to be bought and paid for a year or two before there was any possibility of a return from sales.

As a consequence, Gutenberg was not able to pay either the principle or the interest on his loans, and Johann Fust brought suit against him for an accumulated total debt of 2,026 guilders. Since Gutenberg had pledged his printing house equipment and supplies as security for the loan, Fust apparently took over the printing house and operated it himself in partnership with Peter Schoeffer, who seems to have been Gutenberg's foreman and who came to be related to Fust not only as a partner but (later) as son-in-law. It is presumed that the partnership of Fust and Schoeffer commenced before the printing of the Bible was quite complete. In any event, they went on later to produce other estimable books, most notably a beautiful Psalter of 1457, and another Bible in 1462.

The career of Gutenberg after the termination of his partnership with Fust is somewhat obscure. He may have been allowed to retain part of the earlier printing equipment. He was given a pension by the Archbishop of Mainz in 1465, and he died in obscurity in 1468, at the age of about sixty-nine.

But Gutenberg was not without honor in his own time. Among the many contemporary references to him as the inventor of printing, perhaps none is more rewarding than a letter by the Rector of the University of Paris, Professor Guillaume Fichet, written on December 31, 1470, and printed in 1471, just a couple of years after Gutenberg's death and only some fifteen years after the Bible was printed. (The fact that Fichet was writing in Latin may have loosed him from inhibitions and encouraged a freedom with superlatives, a freedom to be found in the Latin compositions of many Renaissance writers.) "Not far from the city of Mainz" he wrote, "there appeared a certain Johann whose surname was Gutenberg, who, first of all men, devised the art of printing, whereby books are made, not by a reed, as did the an-

ILLUMINATED INITIAL "P"
ILLUSTRATING KING SOLOMON TEACHING A CHILD
OLD TESTAMENT · BOOK OF PROVERBS

cients, nor with a quill pen, as do we, but with metal letters, and that swiftly, neatly, beautifully. Surely this man is worthy to be loaded with divine honors by all the Muses, all the arts, all the tongues of those who delight in books, and is all the more to be preferred to gods and goddesses in that he has put the means of choice within reach of letters themselves and of mortals devoted to culture. That great Gutenberg has discovered things far more pleasing and more divine, in carving out letters in such a fashion that whatever can be said or thought can by them be written down at once and transcribed and committed to the memory of posterity." The praise is deserved, and these comments can still stand as an epitome of the contribution of the invention of printing to the progress of learning.

PRINTING OFFICE   PAPERMAKER

The illustrations on pages 32–33 are woodcuts made from drawings by Jost Amman. They are reproduced from a book by Hartmann Schopper, printed in Frankfurt in 1568. The methods here portrayed are thought to have been those followed, in general, for several hundred years after the invention of printing.

PRINTING OFFICE, 1568. The two men in the background are setting type ("composing") by selecting the characters from the boxes ("the case") in front of them. The two men in front are operating the printing press: the one on the left is removing a sheet of paper on which two pages have just been printed on one side; the one on the right is using circular pads ("balls") with handles to ink the type for two pages. In the foreground, on the left there is a stack of sheets that have already been printed, and on the right a stack of blank sheets of paper.

PAPERMAKER, 1568. The man is dipping a frame or mold of interwoven wires into a vat of smooth pulp. He will raise it from the vat and shake out the water; the wet sheet will then be re-

TYPEFOUNDER

BOOKBINDER

moved from the mold, dried, and pressed. The boy is carrying a stack of finished sheets of paper. Parts of a water mill can be seen in the background; it was used in the process of washing, boiling, and beating linen rags until they became smooth pulp.

TYPEFOUNDER, 1568. The man is pouring molten metal into a mold to form the type. In front of him is a furnace with a fire inside and a bellows leaning against the wall. The metal (an alloy, with lead the main component) was melted on the top of the furnace. The face of the type was formed in a matrix which had been stamped with a hard metal punch.

BOOKBINDER, 1568. The man in the background is sewing together folded sheets that have been printed. The man in the foreground is trimming, with a plow, the uneven edges of a set of sewn sheets. In front of him is a bound book in a hand press. Various tools of the bookbinder's trade are hanging on the wall above the shelf on which there are other books in process.

plenos. Uerba lapientiu ſicut ſtimu-
li: et quaſi claui in altu defixi: que per
magiſtroz conſiliu data ſunt a paſtore
uno. Hijs ampli⁹ fili mi ne requiras.
ſaciendi plures libros null⁹ eſt finis:
frequenſq meditatio carnis afflictio
eſt. ſinem loquendi pariter omnes audi
amus. Deu time: et mandata ei⁹ obſua.
Hoc eſt omnis homo. Cuncta q̃ ſunt
adducet deus in iudiciu pro omni
errato: ſiue bonum ſiue malum ſit.
Explicit eccleſtes ſncipit Catica cã
Oſculet me oſculo o-
ris ſui. Quia melio-
ra ſunt ubera tua ui-
no: fragrātia unge-
tis optimi⁹. Oleum
effuſum nomē tuũ
ideo adoleſcentule dilexerut te. Trahe
me poſt te. Curremus in odore ungueto-
toru tuoz. Introduxit me rex in cella-
ria ſua. Exultabim⁹ et letabim̃ in te:
memores uberu tuoru ſup uinũ. Redi
diligut te. Nigra ſũ ſed formoſa filie
iheruſalē: ſicut tabernacula cedar: ſicut pelles ſalomonis. Nolite me con-
ſiderare tp fuſca ſim: qa decolorauit
me ſol. Filij matris mee pugnauerut
cõtra me: poſuerut me cuſtode uineis.
Uineã meam nõ cuſtodiui. Indica
michi que diligit aĩa mea: ubi paſcas
ubi cubes i meridie: ne uagari incipia
poſt greges ſodaliu tuoz. Si ignoras
te o pulcerrima inter mulieres: egredere
et abi poſt ueſtigia greguu: et paſce hedo
tuos iuxta tabernacula paſtoz. Equi-
tatui meo i curribz pharaonis: aſſimi-
laui te amica mea. Pulcre ſunt gene
tue ſicut turturis: collum tuũ ſicut mo-
nilia. Murenulas aureas faciemus
tibi: uermiculatas argento. Cũ eſſet rex i
accubitu ſuo: nardus mea dedit odorē

ſuũ. ſaſcicul⁹ mirre dilect⁹ me⁹ michi:
inter ubera mea comorabit. Botrus
cipri dilect⁹ meus michi: in uineis en
gaddi. Ecce tu pulcra es amica mea:
ecce tu pulcra: oculi tui colũbaz. Ecce
tu pulcer es dilecte mi: et decor⁹. Lectul⁹
noſter florid⁹: tigna domoz noſtraz
cedrina: laquearia noſtra cipreſſina.
Ego flos campi: et liliũ con-
uallu. Sicut liliũ inter ſpinas:
ſic amica mea inter filias. Sicut mal⁹
inter lingua ſiluaz: ſic dilectus meus
inter filios. Sub umbra illius quem
deſideraueram ſedi: et fructus ei⁹ dulcis
gutturi meo. Introduxit me rex i cella
uinaria: ordinauit in me caritatem.
ſulcite me floribz: ſtipate me malis:
quia amore langueo. Leua ei⁹ ſub capite meo: et dextera illius amplexabit
me. Adiuro uos filie iheruſalem: per
capreas ceruoſq camporũ: ne ſuſcitet
neq uigilare faciatis dilectā: quoad
uſq ipſa uelit. Uox dilecti mei. Ecce
iſte uenit ſaliens in montibz: trãſiliens
colles. Similis eſt dilectus me⁹ capree
hynnuloq ceruoz. En ipſe ſtat poſt
parietē noſtru: reſpiciens per feneſtras:
proſpiciens per cancellos. En dilectus
meus loquit michi. Surge propera
amica mea: columba mea: formoſa
mea et ueni. Iam cũ hiemps tranſijt:
imber abijt et receſſit. Flores apparu-
erunt in terra: tps putacionis aduenit.
Uox turturis audita eſt in terra nõa:
ficus protulit groſſos ſuos: uinee flo-
rentes dederũt odorē ſuũ. Surge propera amica mea ſpecioſa et ueni: columba mea in foraminibus petre in
cauerna maceric. Oſtende michi facie
tuã: ſonet uox tua i auribz meis. Uox
enim tua dulcis: et facies tua decora.
Capite nobis uulpes paruulas: que

ILLUMINATED INITIAL "O"
BEGINNING OF THE SONG OF SOLOMON
OLD TESTAMENT

❧III❧

The Gutenberg Bible Today

THE SURVIVAL rate of copies of the Gutenberg Bible has been high. Today, more than five hundred years after publication, forty-eight copies are recorded: of these, thirty-six are printed on paper and twelve on vellum. If the estimate is correct that the total number originally printed was one hundred and seventy-five copies (one hundred and thirty-five on paper, forty on vellum), the overall survival rate is about one in four, or one in three for those on vellum. (There are, in addition, many fragments and separate leaves which are not usually counted as copies.) Some of these forty-eight copies are not complete, however. Two of the complete copies belonging to libraries in Germany, not seen since World War II, have recently reappeared in Russia. But to return to forty-eight, the total of the complete copies, the incomplete copies, and the missing copies. These are distributed around the world in the United States, Germany, Great Britain, France, Spain and Italy, Japan, Portugal, Switzerland, Austria, Denmark, Belgium, and Poland. Of the copies in the United States three are on vellum (two of them complete), at the Library of Congress, the Pierpont Morgan Library, and the Huntington; of the remaining copies on paper, only four are complete. The Huntington copy is the only copy on the west coast. (Our copy actually lacks two leaves, the last in each volume, which were supplied in facsimile before 1825.) The first copy to come to this country was bought for $2,600 at auction in London on March 13, 1847, for James Lenox of New York; that copy, on paper, is now in the New York Public Library.

Copies do move around occasionally, though it would take both a great deal of patience and money to get a copy. Since the

Huntington copy was acquired in 1911, a number of copies have changed hands (most recently in 1987); all but two or three have found their way into institutional libraries, either by gift or purchase, and presumably the other private copies are in due course destined for institutional ownership. Many copies have been in libraries for centuries; the University of Leipzig, for example, has had its copy since at least 1543. Originally, most of the copies were housed, presumably, in the libraries of monasteries, churches, and ecclesiastical bodies. A copy now in the Bibliothèque Nationale in Paris belonged, as early as 1457, to the church in Ostheim; it is also distinguished by being inscribed with the earliest date that appears on any copy—24 August 1456 on the first volume and 15 August 1456 on the second volume, the dates on which the rubricator (Henricus Cremer) completed his work.

The Huntington copy, which includes both the Old and the New Testaments, is one of the twelve copies on vellum known to exist. It is imposing in physical appearance: it is bound in two massive volumes; together, they weigh fifty–three and a quarter pounds, suitable for the weightiness of the contents. Ours is one of nine copies recorded as being in fifteenth-century bindings. The wooden boards in the binding of our copy are thought to be part of the original, uniform binding of the two volumes done between 1455 and 1460, though the leather covering the boards was renewed in the early sixteenth century. The covers are stamped with a design, and early index tabs (in faded red) are attached to leaves beginning the several books of the Bible to indicate their location. Somewhat later, metal clasps were added to keep each volume closed, and

BLACK LETTER TYPE
OF THE GUTENBERG BIBLE

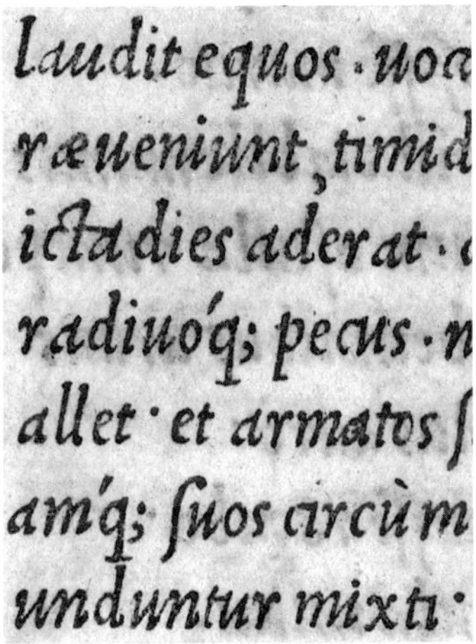

laudit equos · uoc
ræueniunt, timid
icta dies aderat · (
radiuoq; pecus · n
allet · et armatos f
amq; fuos arcùm
unduntur mixti ·

penfa funiculo c(
um allio crudo fu
llūt. Atq₃ in totu
uertigines. Item
cis iniecta:et mo
rpentium ictus u
bus occurrit. Alb
nē facrū. Sine ole

STATIUS'S *SYLVARUM*
LIBRI QUINQUE PRINTED IN
VENICE IN 1502.
An early use of italic type.

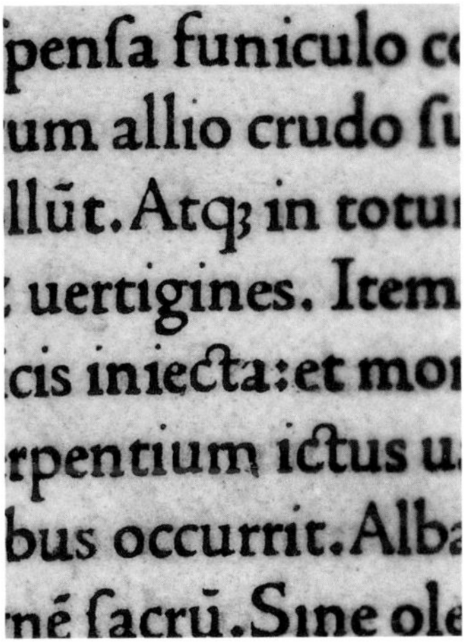

PLINY'S *NATURAL HISTORY*,
PRINTED IN LATIN BY NICHOLAS JENSEN
IN 1472 IN VENICE.
An early use of roman type.

metal bosses were attached to the outside of the covers to protect them from wear and damage.

The leaves of our copy are exceedingly bright. The vellum has hardly darkened, even with the passage of more than five centuries, and the ink used for the text is still glossy black. The gothic (or black letter) type is clear, and as legible as such type can be for those who did not early in life come to terms with German script. Several variations of gothic type soon developed, and within the first half century of printing the two other major families of early type—roman and italic—were created. The sample passages reproduced on these pages show how the type of the Gutenberg Bible compares with the type of other famous books that came after it.

ILLUMINATED INITIAL "L"
ILLUSTRATING AN OX, THE SYMBOL OF LUKE
NEW TESTAMENT · PROLOGUE TO THE BOOK OF LUKE

When the Gutenberg Bible had been printed, the sheets were handed over (much as was the case with manuscripts) to specialists who added the decoration by hand. The rubricator did the pen ornamentation in colored ink (particularly red and blue), the illuminator added the gold work and either the illuminator or another artist did the paintings in the margins and in the initial letters. The decorations shine with such rich colors that one can hardly believe they were applied soon after the book was printed and have never since been touched up. The predominant colors are red, blue, and gold. The page headings, the chapter numbers, the chapter initials, and the large initials are in color.

At the beginning of each of the books of the Bible, there is usually an elaborate decoration in color in a margin, with leaves, sprays, birds, animals, and illustrative drawings. Sometimes a margin is full of drawings, as is the inner margin of the first page of the Book of Genesis, which is shown on page 16: God is at the top, in the act of creation; in the panel below are some of the works of creation, the fish of the sea on the fifth day and the beasts of the earth on the sixth day, with the creation of Eve out of Adam as the last act shown. This reproduction deserves, and will repay, careful scrutiny of its details and of its total effect. It is only about one quarter the size of the original, but even so it gives a reasonable idea of this magnificent book. The leaves of the Huntington copy measure about 16¼" tall and 12" wide; it is one of four (the others being in Rome, Tübingen, and Leipzig) that are the largest of all known copies. It is also remarkable for the many marks and smudges on the pages from the process of printing, including fingerprints which may belong to Gutenberg himself.

Most of the books of the Bible have a small drawing in the large initial letter with which the book commences. Job is portrayed with a dog licking his sores, Daniel with toothy lions on either side of him, and the Psalms begin with a picture of King David playing on his harp.

There are many notable decorations in the Huntington copy of the Gutenberg Bible. There is, for example, a hunting scene in which two dogs are chasing their prey all across one lower margin. In the bottom margin of the Book of Proverbs, a peacock has his magnificent tail spread into the shape of a full fan, while a nearby insect—a bee, perhaps—edges toward an open flower. In the left margin beside the Song of Solomon, five different kinds of birds are posed for their portraits on a gracefully stylized branch which has four varieties of flowers. The decorations throughout both volumes are splendid examples of medieval art.

ILLUMINATED INITIAL "P"

AND MARGINAL DECORATIONS

BEGINNING OF THE BOOK OF PROVERBS

OLD TESTAMENT

❧IV❧

Henry E. Huntington's
Copy of the Gutenberg Bible

L ITTLE IS known about the early history of the Huntington
Bible, other than that an early owner was a member of the
Nostitz family of Lepzig, Germany, where the illumination and
binding were executed. Mr. Huntington's copy of the Gutenberg
Bible was acquired in 1911, in a dramatic way and with fascinat-
ing consequences.

This copy had been the property of an important New York
collector, Robert Hoe. He had bought it in 1898, in great secrecy,
from the London dealer, Bernard Quaritch. Hoe sent a hand-
written letter (which is in our collection) to Quaritch offering to
buy it; he was very apologetic, however, because he already owned
a copy on paper. "It seems absurd," he wrote, "for me to have two
copies of so expensive a book, but I would like to own the Vellum
Copy." (This is the true collector's instinct in action.) "Is there any
way," he said, "of getting it here without any one knowing I had
it?" Nobody: not even the Quaritch employees. There was, and he
got it, for $25,000.

This book was the chief item in the Hoe Sale, which took
place in the Anderson Galleries in New York, in April 1911,
after the death of Robert Hoe. The sale catalog tempted all collectors with the following words, in full capitals: "IT IS THERE-
FORE PROBABLE THAT NO OTHER OPPORTUNITY WILL EVER
OCCUR TO OBTAIN A VELLUM COPY OF THIS MONUMENTAL WORK,
THE FIRST IMPORTANT BOOK PRINTED FROM MOVABLE TYPE." On
Monday evening, April 24, the sales room was crowded with dealers and collectors. The most notable European dealers were present, including the Bernard Quaritch whose father had sold the
Bible to Hoe. The auctioneer, Sidney Hodgson, was brought from

London to handle the sale. Joseph Widener, a wealthy collector from Philadelphia, was sitting in the middle of the front row; the firm of Dodd & Livingston was ready for heavy action; and George D. Smith, the dealer who was to bid for Henry E. Huntington, was in place with Huntington at his side.

The crowd was tense with excitement, and applause rippled through the room when the Gutenberg Bible was announced by the auctioneer in his clipped British accent. He asked for an opening bid, and a wag in the back of the room said, "A hundred dollars." Nervous laughter. Dodd & Livingston started the auction at $10,000, and the bidding moved quickly to $31,000, where that firm dropped out. Quaritch's last bid was $33,000. Only Widener and Smith were left. At $41,000, they began to move by five hundreds, and then by two hundreds. Then Smith increased the pace and said "$46,000." "$47,000," replied Widener. "$48,000," countered Smith. There was a perceptible pause, and then Widener said "$49,000." "$50,000," immediately replied Smith, and there was no answer. The auctioneer raised his hammer, held it a moment, and then let it fall. The audience broke into spontaneous applause, so prolonged that A. Edward Newton (a collector who was present) later wrote of it as one of the great moments he had experienced in the auction rooms.

"Let's see the purchaser! Let him stand up," someone shouted, Smith stood up, Widener slipped out of the room almost unobserved, and it was announced that Huntington was the purchaser. Many of those present felt that they were witnessing an epochal event: the highest price ever given for any book ever sold at auction, the unbelievable sum of $50,000, and the national pride of having the event take place in New York with an American as the purchaser.

Not everyone was pleased, however. Some of the European dealers were disgruntled at their lack of success in the sale, and J. P. Morgan's librarian, Miss Belle da Costa Greene, "left the auction room in a huff," according to the newspapers. The prices,

ILLUMINATED INITIAL "O"
BEGINNING OF THE BOOK OF NAHUM
OLD TESTAMENT

ILLUMINATED INITIAL "P"
BEGINNING OF THE BOOK OF JUDGES
OLD TESTAMENT

she declared, "are perfectly ridiculous. They are more than ridiculous—they are most harmful. They establish a dangerous precedent." "The Hoe collection is being sold practically en bloc," she said, to the same man who bought the Gutenberg Bible. "It has hardly been an auction at all," she fumed. "Buyers have come from all over Europe and are getting nothing."

The great news of the sale of the Gutenberg Bible was carried in hundreds of newspapers throughout the United States, from Burlington, Vermont to Phoenix, Arizona, from Birmingham, Alabama to Muncie, Indiana to Denver, Colorado. The typical story ran about six inches and began with an awed declaration of the price; it told a little about the book, a little about Huntington, and made some mention of other early books of interest. It is hard to imagine any bookish event that would today command that kind of attention in what are now styled the public media.

It is even harder to imagine the kind of attention that the sale gained on the editorial pages. It is astonishing that there were, in the course of a few weeks after the sale, just about as many editorials as there had been news stories, and the editorials tended to be longer. There seem to have been more moralists than book collectors among those editorial writers. Almost all of them dwelt on the price, and there was about an equal distribution of sweet and sour in their opinions. One declared, with more hope than logic, that "When Bibles sell for $50,000 it can't be said that Christianity is on the wane." The Louisville *Courier-Journal* sourly asserted that the sum was paid simply "for the gratification of vanity. . . . From the Gutenberg Bible Mr. Huntington can derive not a whit more artistic, literary or spiritual pleasure than he could get from a 50-cent edition or even from a free copy which any kindly-disposed Christian would cheerfully give him."

The San Francisco *Star* condemned the purchase as an anti-humanitarian act, saying that "one empty stomach is of more moment to humanity than many Gutenberg Bibles," but the Chico, California *Enterprise* found a ray of hope, saying that

"Henry E. Huntington will squeeze half way through the needle's eye if the Lord will let him. The day after he paid $50,000 for the Gutenberg Bible he donated $25,000 to the half million dollar Y.M.C.A. fund."

Huntington's newspaper clipping service dutifully supplied him with this vast quantity of clippings, which we still have. We also still have the avalanche of personal letters that descended on him, and to read them (as I have done) is to become aware of the fact that there are many people out there who have pen in hand, eager to write. In this case, everybody had something to sell. I hope that the flavor will come through from one or two brief examples. From the Comfort Sanitary Poultry Farm—"Texas' Largest Baby-chick Hatchery"—in Comfort, Kendall County, Texas, this short classic: "I read in the paper that you are the buyer of that Gutenberg Bible and having in possession an old Bible myself I am asking the favor from you to let me know how I can find out what my bible is worth. It might be I will sell it. The book was printed in 1747 and is bound in hog skin." (It ought to last.) Bibles without number were offered, some having belonged to a grandfather, all "very valuable." He was offered sundry other books, including Pilgrim's Progress in Welsh, six French books printed in 1812, an 1822 volume on dentistry, the 1816 memoirs of James Wilkinson, a Confederate bond, the writings of Josephus, the sermons of John Boys, and a copy of Cowper's poems sent from England with 32 cent postage due. He was also offered a harpsichord, an old leather head rest, a gentleman's inlaid shaving mirror, a pair of antlers "beautifully mounted," an Old English thermometer—once the property of Beowulf, perhaps—a silver watch with Columbus' ships painted on the face, and about a thousand other objects of vertu.

One letter, from Alexander, Kansas, was addressed to Huntington "c/o the late Collis P. Huntington, New York City, New York." Collis had been dead for eleven years, but the letter was delivered—though not, I believe, by the routing called for in the address.

ILLUMINATED INITIAL "E"
BEGINNING OF THE BOOK OF MACCABEES
OLD TESTAMENT • APOCRYPHA

Another letter came direct from Tucson, Arizona, from a friend named Epes Randolph. "Dear Mr. Huntington: I have known for many years that you were sadly in need of the influence imparted by a constant use of Holy Writ, but I did not suppose that on short notice you would feel the need of $50,000 worth of it 'in a bunch.'"

Huntington replied, "My dear Randolph: I certainly should not have paid $50,000 for that Bible if I had not needed it very much, although, as a matter of fact, I found after I had purchased it that I could buy one for 10 cents, the contents of which would probably have done me as much good as the one I have, so you can imagine how chagrined I felt that I had paid $50,000 for one."

In fact, he was not chagrined at all. The Gutenberg Bible gave him intense pleasure, and he delighted in looking at it, in thinking about what it stands for, and in showing it to his guests. It continues to be a delight to visitors, and it is perhaps a greater attraction than is any other single book in the Library.

It is truly a monumental work, a landmark in learning. It deserves our attention and our respect as a worthy symbol of a revolution in our intellectual life.

ILLUMINATED INITIAL "H"
ILLUSTRATING AN EAGLE, THE SYMBOL OF JOHN
NEW TESTAMENT · PROLOGUE TO THE BOOK OF JOHN